ON THE SUBJECT OF FALLEN THINGS

James Kearns is a poet based in Birmingham and Cape Town. His work focuses on experimentation and collaboration and explores how poetry can interact with other art forms. He has been a winner in the Streetcake Magazine Prize for Experimental Writing and was shortlisted for the 2022 Sound of the Year Awards in association with the National Poetry Library. His pamphlet *After Words* featured in Ghost City Press's 2022 Summer Series and his forthcoming project *A Wee Torchlight Bobbing Up and Down* explores depictions of dementia in experimental poetry and publishing. *On the Subject of Fallen Things* is his debut collection of poetry.

BY THE SAME AUTHOR

After Words
(Ghost City Press, 2022)

On the Subject of Fallen Things

JAMES KEARNS

BAD BETTY PRESS

First published in 2023 by Bad Betty Press
Cobden Place, Cobden Chambers, Nottingham NG1 2ED

badbettypress.com

PB ISBN: 978-1-913268-52-7
EPUB ISBN: 978-1-913268-53-4

A CIP record of this book is available from the British Library.

Book design by Amy Acre

Printed and bound in the UK by TJ Books Limited, Padstow, Cornwall
using FSC® Certified paper from responsibly managed forests

Supported using public funding by
**ARTS COUNCIL
ENGLAND**
LOTTERY FUNDED

MIX
Paper from
responsible sources
FSC® C013056

To my parents,

for all they've given me.

On the Subject of Fallen Things

you start every new day with an inventory: a moth,
a cape, a parachute, a coffin, a gun, the wall you built
to mount the gun.

you start every new day with gunfire as salutation.
just to keep a clear conscience (narratively
speaking). the gun will not go back onto the wall
from which it came. you bankrupt yourself with
the postage and packaging costs of mortar. no
one knows why you put this pressure on yourself.
everyone knows you can't shoot a false promise
(narratively speaking). no one knows why you are
so attached to narratively speaking. except that it's
something to do with loose ends. except your chest
tattoo that says *for the sake of…*

around the time we were talking, you

come through waving Chekhov's gun, dropping
Chekhov's bullets on the floor of Chekhov's petrol
station because you're tired and you've been snorting
groundparacetamol to make a toothache you didn't
know was there go away and this of all Tuesdays it's
going to be different because you're less dead than
you will be this time next week and twice as dead as
you will be the week after that. the superhero on duty
looks at you out of deeppandaeyes and says *we both
know it doesn't work that way.* but just because you can
agree on that doesn't mean you are any more likely
to know the way it actually does work, if at all, and so
you keep your mouth quiet when Chekhov's police
come bursting in the door past the Rolos and start to
open Chekhov's fire.

perhaps there is something here about using things

just because they are there

in a botched attempt to square away the world your first
inventory reads:

the writing on the back of hands, half in lists, wearing
away already.

the heads missing rest in a shoulder, waymarks of the
distance between you and all the people you could have
been in love with from far away.

the rain on the car bonnet lit up, a thousand winks maybe
ten thousand: you live the kind of life where it's not that
important to have been able to tell one from the other.

things which do not know their impermanence yet

the woods from which society is built

nor
the home they find in the ruined hinterbuildings of
authority

nor
dreams squared into plastic boxes and left to
tupperwear out

nor
the first moths of summer to crash into your window.

things of permanence

as a human
you
feel
it
would be
disingenuous
to
think
that
there
could be
anything to say here.

things that do not know their permanence

molecules
recycling

in this night you are making, your babies are
rectangles drawn in haste so hasty that their hands
cannot keep up with their thoughts. this is the only
way to get things done. this is the only way of living a
life where your regrets cannot keep up with you. you
ask yourself questions of existence, of youth, of what
these things can mean when you are not a part of
them anymore. you think of a day when you are not
alive and tell everyone you can comprehend what this
means and do yourself the favour of never examining
this with micro or telescope. you set store by stars and
palms and entrails and this too is a form of knowing
and not knowing of knowing and unknowing of
control and things you could not wish to control.

perhaps there is something here about using things

just because they are there

we swallow things then swallow the fingersdownthroat
that follow. just for good measure. *when you use the gun,*
a sense of inevitability is to be expected the meditation
on cassette tape tells you in a voice drooping from
overplayback. you imagine words dripping off the
speaker's moustache like cave water off a stalactite (goes
down), like your brain down the sides of the rhyme to
remember which one's a stalactite (goes down). read
this like a book, learn / unlearn / try translating a
scream into the paper, at least it might crumple or blow
away. whatever it is, worry it like a wisdom tooth with
your grandma's pliers you took for an inheritance. your
grandma always had a look of Chekhov about her. you
are stinging with tired eyes are gone somewhere your
ears...

because a shroud and a cape are interchangeable,
it is suggested you choose a colour that can work
for both. for this reason Chekhov blue came to
prominence. those remembering wombs thought that
if that beforeness had a colour it might be Chekhov
blue. the things that were Chekhov blue to him
were things he couldn't remember if he was seeing
or feeling. Chekhov blue sounded like someone
bringing their wheelie bin down the street at night,
sounded like the inch before a neighbour's closed
eyelid. Chekhov blue in the relief of someone else's
toilet flushing at the third attempt. Chekhov blue of
the rabbit with its foot still intact. Chekhov blue and
cold played across his lips like a harmonica. Chekhov
blue the colour of bedsheets. Chekhov blue the taste
of pub crisps. Chekhov blue moving up between
knotted shoulders. Chekhov blue warm as the sun
you are worrying your skin with. Chekhov blue in
signatures you don't recognise as your own. Chekhov
blue for what it's worth; it's not worth this.

you can make a tongue form from any crowd of people
if you don't worry what that tongue will say. you can
tongue proverbs till the cows come home. milk idioms
(for all they are worth), (they are worth more than this).
once you believe in Chekhov your tongue will come
back in the shape of a prayer which by all the strains
of logic you ought to have forgotten by now. here
inevitability will start to undo itself like a clairvoyant
who knows he's faking but can't get anyone else to see
it. set, setting, unsettling. you make things fall from the
sky, you holiday another holiday from yourself that you
couldn't afford to take. when the dipping of your power
comes, think not of me, think of what I meant. chew
something for tomorrow brings tomorrow brings just
bringing and you can't understand what this means.

yet yet yet what makes narrative tension a kind of joke is once the gun's on the wall we already know why it's to come off the wall.

veins as apologies, inevitable as a favour given in return.
veins laid out across an arm like planes around a terminal.
like something squaring up to be terminal. like term's
end, like a summer braced to start against a school gate,
like a summer wearing itself out in the first week. like a
child wearing out its first lifetime, the first of all possible
lifetimes; one you're committed to, have fucked up and
can't put down until you've put right. you've heard it said
that you should always leave somewhere better than you
found it. and this sentiment maybe extends to picnic areas,
village halls but none of the important places like planets
or public toilets.

though perhaps there is something here about using things

just because they are there

because a saint and a superhero are functionally
interchangeable, it was suggested epithets might be
used in much the same way for both. for this reason
Google sagged under the weight of searches for
something novel:

the astonishing *(taken)* the evangelist *(taken)*
the navigator *(taken)* the stylite *(taken)* the great
(taken many times over) the confessor *(taken)* the
wonderworker *(taken)* the iconographer *(taken)* the
martyr *(taken)* the obscure *(Hardy)* the redeemer *(Rio)*
the fool *(too similar to fool for Christ)* the fortunate
the reticent the ambitious the vengeful the half-
way the singular the unrequiter the apologist the
pasteurised the trialled the discarded the lamented the
barefoot the toothless the naked the tacit the almost
the coward the sure-footed the clean-handed the
crouched the unstuck the parabolic the innocent the
naïve the innocent the inexistent

you start each memorial service with an inventory of
things that are inevitable. the inventory resembles a
prop list of whatever act has just come before and so
you begin to sound like you are speaking for the sake
of speaking.

perhaps there is something here about prayers

the parabolic the innocent the naïve the innocent
the inexistent *another piece of* the moth-eaten the
defrocked *wisdom intent on* the fallen the sealed the
locked the unloaded the half-cocked *losing teeth*
the knowing the not-knowing the knowing the
unknowing *names supposed to be* the missed the carrier
the carrion *biodegradable as* the styrofoam the plastic
the full *the national anthem of a weekend* the barbarian
the citizen the useful the clicking *stuck to them* the
groaning the drowning *as a shroud imperishable* the
waning *in all the places* the innocent the inexistent
they could not stop existing the indestructible the
indestructible

and so we were left with the corpse of a superhero
and no instructions. we thought that the burying of
him might set the world off its axis. he never burned
when he was alive so why would he burn now? the
undertakers wouldn't take him and he'd been in the
front room so long and to all of our eyes there wasn't
any sign of decay yet. under the breath of thoughts
we asked what was the danger of the radioactivity
leaking out. we were left with the corpse of the
superhero and every night was like a wake. a wake
that keeps on going is called insomnia, we offered as
a hamstrung joke. every night we'd talk about his lack
of relatability and how this corpse was so heavy and
we'd take turns trying to lift it.

on the subject of fallen things

moths drop from the ceiling and that this no longer
says plague to you, you take to be another part of
your religious brain come off in your hands. clay
breaks the clay. so find a stone tomb in which to seal
it. say the prayer that

nobody remembers at its entrance. each tongue a
mass extinction then look to Lazarus: patron saint
of walking into the wrong light. the moths flock to
him but he offers only something prosaic by way
of explanation. he has been on the wrong side of a
miracle too. the article of faith subject to a life sat in
the pub with no one believing him. when eventually
he showed them the newspaper clippings, rumours of
cannibalism followed him everywhere.

perhaps there is something here about doing for the sake of doing

it's widely concluded that with all narrative developments having been telegraphed in the previous act, the future must likewise be announcing itself non-stop in the present. all it takes is to look and for this reason clairvoyance becomes flavour of the month.

the psychic tells you that he doesn't think it works that way.

you tell him as all narrative developments have been telegraphed in the previous act, the future must likewise be announcing itself non-stop in the present so all it takes is to look and he is forced to admit he struggles with details and besides hasn't been paying that close attention.

yet yet yet what makes tension a kind of joke (narratively speaking) is that when the generalised fear meant the wall came down, the gun stayed suspended in the air. and what were we to think but that it was so unforgivably light, else the atmosphere heavy beyond reason?

it's widely thought that superheroes seem so few because
the number that die out unfullyformed and bedding in
their powers is frankly overwhelming. the superhero's
fontanelle period

which, let's have some perspective, is always somewhat
inevitable. yes, please let's have perspective,

you cannot expect the chance of survival for something
still becoming to be anything but this.

even with rabbit feet you cannot outrun the white
sheet under which a person wakes up and knows they
are dead. if they are lucky, their first thoughts settle
not over family / friends / missed opportunity but
on words learned by rote from a voice drooping from
overplayback. if they are lucky and coincidence has not
cut their throat.

a person under sheet might long for twitch or stretch or
blood to flow again; a recolouring. to tense and untense
one last time before the ground rises up and they realise
how very different that is to the road rising up. you'd
always taken that for a mistranslation anyway. regardless,
the ground will come to meet you, will stretch far
enough to reach over you, you always thought it would
be warm, that what was inevitable would also be simple.

in a botched attempt to square away the world your first
apologia reads:

and what we mean by cannibalism is that the hand that
feeds won't come from above.

and what we mean by cannibalism is that no one rides
on a back forever without wondering.

and what we mean by cannibalism is that the footprints on the shoulders on which you're standing are not as off-putting as they should be.

in the refuge of breath again. each one made equal
and irregular as allotment plots. even under the shelter
of self-made clouds, a home from home is not a
home. the wake that keeps on going swirls parachute
thoughts above you; the parachutists guiding them,
inconsequential, slumbering. in the furry fury of the
last moments of being awake come all the thoughts
that you needed today rushing to meet a deadline.
this act's end just a chasing away of tomorrow; empty-
handed a day as it will be the one time you need
it. a self-replicating algorithm spinning on in the
background.

perhaps there is something here about doing for the sake of doing

just bandanas waving in the wind; you didn't mean
any of it. yet apologies come like licks of an ice
cream, quicker to stop the melt. wear summer lightly.
trust that insects won't always be there to plague
you through your nights. feel summer breathe. feel a
breath to be an instrument of life and nothing more.
no warmth no sigh no harbinger of forgiveness. wear
summer heavy. feel the embarrassment of clouds sink
the horizon; debris of a day caught out by never
being as nice as it threatened. it's not its fault but it's
always someone's fault and someone will say sorry
for a summer they never could have stopped existing.

yet yet yet what makes tension a kind of joke is that
more than anything a person is a collective effort of
willing into being

and this only becomes apparent

when someone lets the slack in from their end.

guardian of what? since there came a generalised fear
of having to use things once they existed, a world
happened without walls and so barbarians passed
without opposition and they stopped calling barbarian
and started calling them people, calling them citizens
but only long after they had started calling when they
needed something. the superhero would say *you often
forget what I was before I was your neighbour; in much the
same way as you often forget what you were before you were
a person.*

you forget like you know how convenient forgetting
is. next time you are stuck on the night like a moth
drying on a bathroom tile: call barbarian call out
barbarian call again and pretend you don't recognise a
kind of Chekhov in the mirror.

perhaps there is something here about what 'the sake of' is

yet yet yet should it come to the question of unrealistic
expectations

      we should look to him, the blue showing through
          him like tomorrow's stubble through a cheek.

gun to head, anyone might break and pray to a superhero

for pains you do not know how to feel. for routines you cannot escape. for ink that deserts you. for passion that masquerades as play. for a life that is never where you left it. for woods full of sticks you could build anything from. for the fortune you are going to make of yourself always. for *always* the concept of which you wear as a brooch. for all your todays. for all your tomorrows. for those being the same set of days in a way you can't quite square. for this to be what you'd keep in the locket. for the power to be yourself unselfconsciously. for forever to be an untelling.

(an algorithm here hears a somewhere set to work)

eat the hand eat the wrist eat the above eat the back eat
the shoulders eat the plate eat the continuity error eat
the should have been eat the grief eat the dinner eat the
inevitable eat the difference eat the grief eat the grief eat
the grief eat the grief eat the grief eat

since there came a generalised fear that things would
only come into existence for their later purpose, Google
sagged under the weight of searches into the meaning of
ingrown hairs:

a fossil of one's self
embedded

an excommunication gone wrong

every prayer
bit back on

and so perhaps there is something to speaking for the
sake of speaking.

in pyjama feet you whisper the night you are making back into wellness: its magnet noises drawing all sound to the stubbing of a toe. you invest in the resulting silence like it will pay you back. you buy into its ambiguities. you won't say what your name was. in the night you wear darkness like a belt. too tight. like a hooded cape. like evening dress you have sewn yourself into. in the middle of a summer night you shiver not just because you are cold but because you remember at last what it is to be warm.

inhaling plastic; in time, just the memory of plastic: now you know how the fish feel. at the bottom of the sea you'll store fears in shipwrecks. hope the currents drag them away to wash up on someone else's continent. but the sea is weak against memory and nothing else, so it sits there like an undigested wardrobe in the stomach of a snake. it fragments, trickles up food chains that only ever lead back to you. you are cursed like an apex predator. you'd much rather be a small fish or a piece of plastic; temporary or indestructible but, vitally, unaware of either.

the psychic says *we both know it doesn't work that way.*
but, given the insistence, eventually asks: *well, how are*
you afraid it will happen?

that I will piss myself away

that I will self-deprecate myself out of existence

accidental ingestion of household chemicals, if only to
have justified all the anxiety in the previous acts

the psychic says *perhaps there is something here about*
speaking into existence.

and perhaps there is something here about speaking into existence

(as if to the assembly)

he had often complained of drowning in plastic KAPOWs
and #alltheotherthingshecouldntsquarewithbeingasuperhero.
admiring looks, tight clothes, responsibility. a cape is a noose
that has come open at one end. the longer it went on the
more he began to wonder when he would be forced to go
live in the woods somewhere making no noise (a death to
someone who can't fully grasp the concept of death).

(as if...)

he was in that café, talking to the woman whose husband
he'd been five minutes late to save and his words then
weren't superhero words and his cape kept getting tangled
in his chair and he didn't really drink coffee or like the
taste of it but if the spoon kept moving it would all keep
moving and when he patted her on the shoulder, his hand
was heavy beyond reason.

and what we mean by cannibalism

is from whose plate did Lazarus eat at the continuity error
where his funeral should have been?

the city's fingerprints still there, spaced out in the ash stains
crushed moths leave on your white walls. a thumbmark
on a forehead. the city puts prints on you, over you
sometimes, and you are the one left feeling mothed. when
you leave the city

though you live on its edges, you are
citybrainedurbanbrainedmetrobrainedcitybrained (still
see the first of the trees and think of pencils). when you
hold your own fingerprints up to the city's to prove
your innocence, you notice its are whorls and yours are
a violence laid out in ringroads and street furniture and
lighting that stays on all night to engender a feeling of
safety, tell you where your home is, backlight your chest
tattoo, leave you with an intractable sense of moth.

on the subject of fallen things

how often does a parachutist get back to their family
or empty kitchen and marvel that it's life-sized again?
how often ensconced in family or empty kitchen do
they think of that second where the inevitability of
pulling the cord came loose? so high the fields stitched
together and the people whittled away to nothings.
so high that shooting Chekhov's gun might sound
insignificant.

perspective can be defined as *close enough to see, far
enough that it won't hurt.*

it is perhaps inevitable that we don't use parachutists
for perspective anymore.

on the subject of failing things

I planted an orange tree against the logic of the climate.
a dead grandmother appeared in a dream talking in
poetry that I couldn't hear for the clicking. the existence
of a Chekhov must mean these are connected. gun to
my head, I can't think how.

and what we mean by cannibalism

is that if you are finished with that day, though there
is meat on it still you are too weaktongued to want,

will you shut your eyes and pass it down the table
please?

at the heart of the algorithm that controls it all is control
itself. it bangs fists like a toddler in a high chair and isn't
satisfied with anything small. in the face of the algorithm
that controls it all is a nose growing longer, a moustache
dripping into a pool of noises you don't mention. you
and it both knowing it doesn't work

that way. at the foot of the algorithm that controls it
all is an asterisk to who you are once you disregard
the search history. between the shoulder blades of the
algorithm that controls it all there's a knot it works over
but never resolves, until you wonder if a knot isn't just
its personality, your personality by extension. a knot is a
type of asterisk,

after all. in the caved-in shadow of its control you get
cold, you get pneumonia (go down), start your question
then…

and what we mean by cannibalism

is that if I make my dinner from the discontinuity where
your dinner should be then what comes next is inevitable
and what comes next is to ask *what's the difference?*

a cure for moths. a cure for your phobia of moths; your
skin so white they take you for the moon. a cure for your
love of moths: who having no direction will hurry anyway.

to cure your wanting to be a moth, ask how long you can
push against a bulb to satisfy a case of mistaken identity. if
you can't fudge an answer for this then I can't help you.

and what we mean by cannibalism

is that you should be prepared to eat the grief left behind
as well.

microscope, telescope, a coating of fingerprints, an unwell
orange tree:

you start inventories for the sake of counting. the shape
your tongue comes back as is 42 words. 42 things fallen
from your head in one way or the other; gun to head,
you won't say which.

perhaps there is something to doing for the sake of doing

it would later be recognised as a natural stage in
the development of a superhero that they would
undergo an antisocial period of living in the woods,
eating children etc. it's taken as given that any life
lasting longer than one lifetime will veer towards
cannibalism. upon emerging from this period, many
took the given name *Lazarus*, who was after all the
patron saint of an unasked-for indestructibility.

it's thought the removal of the stigma of apex
predator was a good thing for humans. up to that
point, the entr'acte peril they'd made of plastic was
the only thing left eating at them, yet it is taken as
written that their lifetimes, however grotesque, came
up just short of cannibalism.

a clear demarcation between an act's end and the next
beginning

is key to understanding the teachings of Chekhov.

eat the grief eat the grief eat the grief eat the grief
eat the grief eat the grief eat the grief eat the grief
eat the grief eat the grief eat the grief eat the grief
eat the grief eat the grief eat the grief eat the grief
eat the grief eat the grief eat the grief eat the grief
eat the grief eat the grief eat the grief eat the grief
eat the grief eat the grief eat the grief eat the grief
eat the grief eat the grief eat the grief eat the grief
eat the grief eat the grief eat the grief eat the grief
eat the grief eat the grief eat the grief eat the grief
eat the grief eat the grief eat the grief eat the grief
eat the grief eat the grief eat the grief eat the grief
eat the grief eat the grief eat the grief eat the grief
eat the grief eat the grief eat the grief eat the grief
eat the grief eat the grief eat the grief eat the grief
eat the grief eat the grief eat the grief eat the grief
eat the grief eat the grief eat the grief eat the grief
eat the grief eat the grief eat the grief eat the grief
eat the grief eat the grief eat the grief eat the grief
eat the grief eat the grief eat the grief eat the grief
eat the grief eat the grief eat the grief eat the grief
eat the grief eat the grief eat the grief eat the grief
eat the grief eat the grief eat the grief eat the grief
eat the grief eat the grief eat the grief eat the grief
eat the grief eat the grief eat the grief eat the grief
eat the grief eat the grief eat the grief eat the grief
eat the grief eat the grief eat the grief eat the grief
eat the grief eat the grief eat the grief eat the grief
eat the grief eat the grief eat the grief eat the grief
eat the grief eat the grief eat the grief eat the grief
eat the grief eat the grief eat the grief eat please eat

yet yet yet what makes tension a kind of joke is that
to be the one left is to be the one left holding.

the psychic says *we both know it doesn't work that way.*
but, given the insistence, eventually asks: *what do you
even have to be afraid of?*

the going to the woods

or

the not going to the woods

or

really, I think just the being quiet

the psychic says *I think we are talking for the sake of
talking.*

a sense of termination as is natural in anything. anything living that has lived and known life will stare down a dark corner of not knowing, one day. not to be too philosophical about it, but in most buildings the exit is usually contained in the entrance, a clock starts where it ends, a wave means both hello and I'm never going to see you again. to this end, take verbatim your last words and the absence of your last words and all the unwords that were there instead. unsaid words are a hard concept to square with Chekhov. so take verbatim the whole hospital ward and the impurity of the snow-blanked day and let me wear them in place of shoulder blades. I knot and can't think what will happen when I can't make the memory of you stretch far enough to keep my tea warm and yet there's still the click of your walking and the groan of your knees sounding somewhere near.

perhaps there is something here about things that are not there

yet yet yet should it come to the question of
unrealistic expectations

we should look to him, the blue showing through his
cheeks like tomorrow's uncoming stubble,

        still to drink Chekhov's champagne, still to say
        Chekhov's inevitable last words,

            still it's been so long…

act. unact. unfinish the act. unstart

the next. unsquare the circle. unsquare away the world.
unbotch the last attempt. this chasing away of tomorrow:
an empty wall, an empty table as it may be.

eat the parabolic eat the innocent eat the naïve eat
the innocent eat the inexistent eat the moth-eaten
eat the defrocked eat the fallen eat the sealed eat the
locked eat the unloaded eat the half-cocked eat the
knowing eat the not-knowing eat the knowing eat
the unknowing eat the missed eat the carrier eat the
carrion eat the styrofoam eat the plastic eat the full
eat the barbarian eat the citizen eat the useful eat the
clicking eat the groaning eat the drowning eat the
waning eat the innocent eat the inexistent eat the
indestructible eat the indestructible

eat the plastic eat the plastic eat the plastic eat the
plastic eat the plastic eat the plastic eat the plastic eat
the plastic eat the plastic eat the plastic eat the plastic
eat the plastic eat the plastic eat the plastic eat the
plastic eat the plastic eat the plastic eat the plastic eat
the plastic eat the plastic eat the plastic eat the plastic
eat the plastic eat the plastic eat the plastic eat the
plastic eat the plastic eat the plastic eat the plastic eat
the plastic eat the plastic eat the plastic eat the plastic
eat the plastic eat the plastic eat the plastic eat the
plastic eat the plastic eat the plastic eat the plastic eat
the plastic eat the plastic eat the plastic eat the plastic
eat the plastic eat the plastic eat the plastic eat the
plastic eat the plastic eat the plastic eat the plastic eat
the plastic eat the plastic eat the plastic eat the plastic
eat the plastic eat the plastic eat the plastic eat the
plastic eat the plastic eat the plastic eat the plastic eat
the plastic eat the plastic eat the plastic eat the plastic
eat the plastic eat the plastic eat the plastic eat the
plastic eat the plastic eat the plastic eat the plastic eat
the plastic eat the plastic eat the plastic eat the plastic
eat the plastic eat the plastic eat the plastic eat the
plastic eat the plastic eat the plastic eat the plastic eat
the plastic eat the plastic eat the plastic eat the plastic
eat the plastic eat the plastic eat the plastic eat the
plastic eat the plastic eat the plastic eat the plastic eat
the plastic eat the plastic eat the grief that's made of
plastic

yet, yet, yet what makes rigor mortis a kind of joke
is that more than anything death is an untensing. a
resection of hours from flesh. present and future go
under the shroud

even the past of them whines like a wisdom tooth

then everyone will get a look of Chekhov about them

a gunshot sounds like a somewhere

their lips tinge an inevitable shade of blue.

ACKNOWLEDGEMENTS

Thank you to Amy and Jake at Bad Betty for choosing to publish this collection and working so hard to bring it into being. Thank you, Amy, for the careful consideration and attention you have given to editing the book. Thank you to Roger and Steven for taking the time to read the book and give blurb quotes.

Thank you to Roger, too, for his mentorship, both within the BAIT programme and since its conclusion. Thanks to Beatfreeks for making the BAIT programme happen and to my fellow BAIT members, my art siblings. Thank you to all at Northfield Arts Forum for allowing me to call myself a professional poet for the first time.

Thank you to all within the Birmingham poetry community, without whose thousand small acts of encouragement this book would probably not exist. Thank you especially to those who built the poetry nights and thus the community, particularly to Jess Davies who created both spaces at which I shared poetry for the first time in a group and in front of an audience. Thank you to Artefact for being the host venue for both those platforms and for accommodating my own night too. Thank you to all my fellow Crunch members for countless hours of shared work and ideas, no matter how out-there.

Thank you to my family – at home, in Scotland, and in South Africa – for their endless support and encouragement in the years leading up to this. Thank you, lastly, to Maria, my first reader and my first everything.